The Danny Crowe Show

David Farr is a writer and director. As director he has focused on international work, and was Artistic Director of London's Gate Theatre from 1995 to 1998. Plays he has directed include *Seven Doors*, *The Great Highway*, *The Boat Plays*, *The Barbarous Comedies*, *Candide*, *Danton's Death* and *Leonce and Lena*. His own play *Elton John's Glasses* premièred at Watford Palace Theatre in 1997 and won the Writer's Guild Best New Play award for that season, opening in the West End in 1998. His play for children *The Nativity* premièred at the Young Vic Theatre at Christmas 1999. His play *Crime and Punishment in Dalston* will première at the Arcola Theatre in January 2002. His play *Night of the Soul* will be produced by the RSC in April 2002.

by the same author

ELTON JOHN'S GLASSES
THE NATIVITY

David Farr
The Danny Crowe Show

First published in 2001
by Faber and Faber Limited
3 Queen Square, London WC1N 3AU

Typeset by Country Setting, Kingsdown, Kent CT14 8ES
Printed in England by Intype London Ltd

All rights reserved

Copyright © David Farr, 2001

David Farr is hereby identified as author
of this work in accordance with Section 77 of the
Copyright, Designs and Patents Act 1988

All rights whatsoever in this work are strictly reserved.
Applications for permission for any use whatsoever including
performance rights must be made in advance, prior to any such
proposed use, to Peters Fraser and Dunlop, Drury House,
34–43 Russell Street, London WC2B 5HA (www.pfd.co.uk).
No performance may be given unless a licence
has first been obtained

*This book is sold subject to the condition that it shall not, by
way of trade or otherwise, be lent, resold, hired out or otherwise
circulated without the publisher's prior consent in any form of
binding or cover other than that in which it is published and
without a similar condition including this condition being
imposed on the subsequent purchaser*

A CIP record for this book
is available from the British Library

ISBN 0-571-21507-6

2 4 6 8 10 9 7 5 3 1

*We're not happy and we can't be happy:
we only want happiness*

Anton Chekhov

The Danny Crowe Show, commissioned by the Ambassadors Theatre Group and Act Productions, premièred at the Bush Theatre, London, on 10 October 2001. The cast was as follows:

Lynette Selina Chilton
Tiffany Lisa Ellis
Miles Tom Goodman-Hil
Magda Clare Holman
Peter Mark Rice-Oxley
Roger Tony Turner

Directed by Dominic Hill
Designer Tom Piper
Lighting Designer Mark Doubleday

Characters

Peter, sixteen
Lynette, seventeen
Magda, thirty-three
Miles, thirty-five
Tiffany, fifteen
Roger, forty-four

Location

A small Cheshire railway town:
corridor in offices of a church, then
the living room in an old railwayman's cottage

Time

The present. A cold, utterly miserable Saturday
in February. Late afternoon. Then evening.

One

SCENE ONE

6.00 p.m. An old, miserable corridor leading to church offices. A row of motley chairs against the wall. A table. A plate of biscuits on the table. A jug of water. A door off the corridor. It has a dust shadow where a large cross once hung. Now it has an ad hoc sign hanging from a nail, 'The Danny Crowe Show – Please Wait Here', scrawled in neurotic handwriting.

Lynette sits on a chair. Peter enters down the corridor, a shy, nervous small sixteen-year-old in an old black coat. Lynette speaks with a Lancashire accent but with a sense of self-improvement. Peter speaks with a soft, hushed, Cheshire accent.

Lynette You here for Danny Crowe?

Pause.

You may as well sit down. They're not in a hurry.

He doesn't.

Lynette What d'you reckon, you think he's here?

Peter Who?

Lynette Danny Crowe.

Peter Oh. I don't know.

Lynette Well, he isn't. We're meeting a minion. Danny only meets the ones that make it to the show. To London. Danny's got no time to bother with people that aren't seriously fucked in the head. Do you think you're fucked in the head?

I

Peter I don't know.

Lynette You look like you could be.

Peter Do I?

Lynette Yeah. Honest.

Peter Thanks.

Lynette Did you watch it last night? 'He was having us all and none of us knew.'

Peter No.

Lynette Six sisters all being given it by the same fella and not one of them twigged. Don't fancy being at their next Christmas. Would have struck me as fishy.

Peter You never know until you're in a situation. What you might see. What you might not.

Lynette (*impressed*) I suppose that's right. We're unpredictable aren't we? I am. (*eating a biscuit*) Want a Dodger?

Peter No thank you.

Lynette You from round here?

Peter Live out by the cemetery.

Lynette Near those scrubby little cottages?

Peter In one. The last in the row.

Lynette The tiny one on the railway line? Thought that was derelict. I had a wee round the back of there once.

Pause.

I'm from Bury originally. That's part of my story for Danny.

Pause.

Do you want to hear my story for Danny?

Peter If you like.

Lynette Promise to keep it confidential? I mean I shouldn't tell you at all . . .

Peter I promise.

Lynette Well, I was down the youth club with Sarah and Michelle and we were just saying how all the boys in Bury were like such stiffs and not worth our time? And this fella comes in and like a flash I know that he's special. Well, he's taking a casual look around and his gaze alights on me, like on a branch, so for dinner, he takes me to this nice quiet place, very classy, wine and cheese and that, and he's got these eyes. And he's saying I could be this and I could be that, the world is my oyster, that's his view. Well I've always been impulsive by nature. I dump Derek, tell me ma I'm leaving – she's pleased enough to see the back of me, I'm not easy – and move into Charlie's loft apartment in Oldham, his name's actually Charlton, after Charlton Heston, but he prefers Charlie. Charlie becomes my manager. He sets me up with a few auditions and the like. I'm doing all right, I've done a couple of car shows, one in London, Lower Barnet, and a bit of dancing in a club as cover for another of the girls on Charlie's books, but nothing surefire. After a while I go to Charlie and say, Charlie let's not pull our punches I am not breaking through here. Charlie takes a long hard look at me and says, girl you've not got enough up top. My chest he means. I read when I can. Charlie says if I'm going to make it, I've got to turn a B minus into an A double-plus. He says he'll pay for the op, he knows a fella in South Shields who'll do it cheap. I get the bus over the Pennines. Charlie's going to come with me but he gets waylaid by a last minute hubbub on the business side. I meet the surgeon, and he's such a pro. He tells me about all the stars he's done – it's amazing who he's done, I can't name names, because if I became a star I'd feel the same way. He's just finished the first one when the phone rings. It's Charlie. He's phoning to say stop the op – his business has gone down. In actual fact he's gone down, he's in Manchester police station answering some questions. The surgeon says he's sorry but he can't do the other one, all he can do is take the first one out again. That's when a girl gets to thinking . . . They've never had a one-implant girl on the Danny Crowe show. I reckon it's a unique selling point.

Peter Which one is it?

Lynette Can't you tell?

Peter Uh . . . the left one. The left one . . . has it.

Lynette No, it's the right one.

Peter Oh. I see now.

Lynette It's the bra. It equals it out. In the flesh it's as clear as day. What's your unique selling point?

Peter It's different to yours.

Lynette Well, I imagine it is.

Peter It's a long story.

Lynette Not too long I hope. Switches viewers off.

Peter I think I'd rather not tell you.

Lynette Suit yourself. You're a rival anyway . . . oh, go on.

Pause.

Lynette You all right? D'you want a pill? I've got some.

Peter No I just need to . . .

Lynette Get it off your chest.

Pause. He looks at her with sudden urgent clarity.

Peter I think I just killed my father.

Pause.

Lynette Oh wow.

Peter Yeah.

Lynette You killed your pa.

Peter Yeah.

Lynette What did your ma say?

Peter She's dead. I didn't kill her. She died anyway.

Lynette You killed your pa. Oh my God. You killed your pa. You're a killer.

Peter I am.

Lynette No, but killing your pa. I mean we've all thought about it. But actually killing your pa. Listen . . .

Peter Peter.

Lynette Lynette. Nice to meet you, Peter.

Peter Likewise.

Lynette How did you do it?

Peter With a knife.

Lynette Oh wow.

Peter Yeah.

Lynette Did he fight?

Peter Oh yeah.

Lynette He was a big man.

Peter Colossal.

Lynette Broad-shouldered like a lion. Did he beat you?

Peter Unmercifully.

Lynette And tore a strip off you at every opportunity.

Peter . . .

Lynette Until one day, Peter, you couldn't stand for it any more.

Peter . . .

Lynette You stood up and you faced your fear!

Pause. Peter reaches for a biscuit.

Lynette This bra does disguise the difference doesn't it?

Peter (*his mouth full*) It's a shame.

Lynette Maybe I should take it off for the interview . . .

Peter (*his mouth still full*) If that's your . . .

Lynette (*suddenly up and to him*) Unique selling point. You have the most amazing eyes.

Peter Yours are blue.

Lynette Like a foreign sky.

Peter Have you been abroad?

Lynette Charlie has. It was his comparison.

Pause. Lynette looks at her breasts and gets up.

Lynette Wait there, murderer . . .

She leaves down the corridor. Peter immediately runs to the Danny Crowe door and knocks. Magda comes out. She is dressed in ripped combat trousers, fingerless gloves and two jumpers, and her hair is roughly cropped short. She has no make-up on and looks pale. She has a mobile phone in one hand, and in the other a huge file, to which she is referring.

Magda (*to the phone*) I am sorry, there is nothing I can offer your daughter . . . (*She sees Peter. Beat. To the phone.*) I know she had high hopes, Mr Miller. It's not that she's not fat enough, she's very fat, we're just not doing fat this series. Her getting even fatter would not change anything, no. (*She puts the phone down.*) Peter? What is it?

Peter Something's happened. Back at the house.

Magda Are you all right?

He shakes his head. Magda puts down her file and holds him.

Oh you poor boy. You poor boy. (*She holds him and strokes his hair.*) Why don't you – (*Kisses his hair.*) – come inside and tell me all about it?

Peter nods. They enter the room together and close the door.
Enter Miles. He looks around. Sees the sign scrawled on the door. Sees the file. He leafs through the hundreds of pages. Stands amazed. Puts file back on the chair. He approaches the door and knocks gently.

Miles Magda, are you in there? (*He tries the door. It is locked.*) Magda, come out please. I know you're there.

The door opens just a little bit.

Magda Miles. Could you come back later?

Miles I've just spent four months looking for you. Would you please let me in!

Magda comes out and shuts the door behind her. She sees and takes file. Pause.

Magda I know what you're thinking.

Miles You look . . .

Magda Different. I had an urge for a change.

Miles Who did that to your hair?

Magda I did.

Miles And those clothes?

Magda I've lost weight. Everything was hanging off me.

Miles How much have you lost?

Magda I don't know. Three stone maybe. I don't have a scale. I wish you'd warned me you were coming.

Miles I would love to have.

Magda I would have prepared.

Miles But your mobile has been switched off for four months.

Beat.

Magda I changed the number. I needed to disappear for a while.

Miles Have you any idea how worried I've been?

Magda I left a message every week with my mother.

Miles Why didn't you call me?

Magda I told Mum to call you.

Miles But you didn't think it was worth calling me yourself.

Magda You knew I was going away.

Miles For a week!

Magda I never said for sure . . .

Miles A week in Bootle!

Magda I know but . . . !

Miles A week's research in Bootle to find Danny some serious underbelly!

Beat.

Magda It didn't work out in Bootle.

Miles It also didn't work out in Preston, Burnley, Bolton, Oldham, Rochdale or Leigh did it?

Pause.

Magda How did you know that?

Miles I traced you. You left a trail of pain behind you, as you sashayed from mill-town to mill-town. You left witnesses. The Rochdale plumber with his dying dog. The Blackburn telephonist with the skin complaint. The crack dealer from Leigh. All remember you with great affection. If my research is correct you started on Merseyside, headed into Lancashire, took in a brief tour of the Wirral and then continued down into North Cheshire. You arrived here in late November, offering succour to the poor and needy for three days from your base at the Travelodge. After that I lost you. The trail went cold. I tried neighbouring towns. I tried further afield. Nothing. Until this morning. I found this. (*He holds up a piece of newspaper, a small advert.*) 'Raw pain required. No one refused. The Church of St Mary. Side entrance. Come any time except Sunday a.m.'

Pause.

How long have you been holed up here?

Magda Two months. I needed to take root. I'd been travelling too much, I'd lost all sense of where I was. It's so easy to become dissipated when working like this.

Miles Why not stay at the Travelodge?

Magda It wasn't right.

Miles Not comfortable?

Magda Too comfortable. I couldn't connect with people.

Miles So where are you sleeping?

Magda Around.

Miles Around where?

Pause.

You're sleeping in there?

Magda I have a mattress. Running water.

Miles Heating?

Magda I have some blankets the sexton gave me. I find it easier to get to grips with people if I live on site. I need that immediacy. It's been very successful, I've had a much higher attendance rate since the move.

Miles How high?

Magda I mean it's hard to say. I would have to estimate. Two thousand?

Miles Magda, that's the whole town.

Magda There are a lot of problems round here. Even the vicar came to talk about his depression. He's losing his congregation. He said he'd kill to get the kind of numbers I'm seeing.

Miles And yet not one of these stricken souls have you sent to Danny.

Magda I just haven't found anything that's really grabbed me.

Miles Four months, Magda. Fifteen towns!

Magda I'm working on it!

Miles This is the North West. This is high-yield terrain.

Magda Underbelly doesn't pop up on every street corner. You need to worm it out.

Miles Larushka was in Walsall for three days. She got a heroin baby and an Asian transexual.

Magda My standards have risen since I've been here. If I don't feel it then I don't think anyone else will.

Miles Magda this is television.

Magda I haven't felt it.

Miles You don't have to feel it.

Magda I do!

Miles You just have to make it! (*Beat.*) Danny was for sacking you after three weeks of this jaunt.

Magda Why didn't he?

Miles Maybe because some daft sucker said he would produce your shows as well as his. It's not easy to find that amount of horror every week. I've had to be fucking resourceful.

Magda I'm sure you've managed.

Miles Yes, I have. In fact I have a very interesting live special this Monday. A pair of obese twins. But that is not to say it's been easy.

Magda I'm very grateful.

Miles Sixteen hour days doing nothing but meeting people with their endless fucking tragedies, and then dashing up here every weekend to try and find my fucking girlfriend!

Magda You didn't have to do that.

Miles What did you expect me to do? Give up on you?

Beat.

Magda You look tired.

Miles It gets to a man. Bed. Weirdos. Bed. Weirdos. I missed you.

Magda Did you?

Miles Of course I did.

He tries to embrace her. She uses the folder as a shield. Pause.

Right.

Magda Sorry.

Miles No, it's fine.

Magda It's nothing to do with . . .

Miles Not a problem.

Magda It's just not where I am right now.

Miles Right. (*Beat.*) Show me that.

Magda What?

Miles That thing you stuck in my ribs. The Domesday Book.

She hands him it. He leafs through it, then alights on something.

Miles OK. Jenny Billick. Domestic abuse. Why didn't you feel that?

Magda We've done abuse a thousand times. It's lost all impact.

Miles Not if there's a twist.

Magda There wasn't.

Miles Laura Gishley. Multi-personalities. How many?

Magda Twelve, she claimed. Most of them fictional. All of them dull.

Miles The Phillipses. Narcoleptic?

Magda So they say.

Miles The whole family?

Magda So what? It just makes car trips tricky. (*Beat.*) I found one man. He'd had his ribs taken out, on a whim. He did shows about it in a pub. Called himself the great ribless miracle.

Miles What happened?

Magda He died.

Miles Magda, I understand that the purity we seek is increasingly difficult to find.

Magda They're on to us. They come in advertising their fuck-ups like cereal.

Miles Nonetheless we have to have product.

Magda Everywhere I go it's the same. They think they can swan in sporting a broken arm or a busted marriage and hey presto – it's showtime. Even the vicar here – milking his loss of faith for all it was worth. Wanking on about the deafening silence of God, giving me those cow eyes. What does anyone these days know about real feeling, real pain?

Miles I should never have got you this job.

Magda I love this job.

Miles You're not right for it. You haven't got the requisite pragmatism.

Magda Nihilism.

Miles Irony! You can't afford to believe in things so much. You're too idealistic.

Magda That's nonsense.

Miles You should have stuck with your documentaries.

Magda No one saw my documentaries.

Miles They were remarkable pieces of work. The short about the decline of the Latvian hill shepherds . . .

Magda Was enjoyed by you, me and three Latvian shepherds.

Miles Does that matter?

Magda I will not die big in Riga.

Miles I want you to come back with me.

Magda I can't.

Miles Magda, you need help.

Magda I need to be left alone.

Miles To do what? To go awol once more?

Magda I am doing really important work here . . .

Miles Where are you going to try next? Where is the holy grail of pain truly to be found?

Magda If you just let me be . . .

Miles I am trying to help you here.

Magda I am really close to getting something!

Miles Is it Danny you're worried about? Listen, we'll take something from the book, jazz it up a bit . . .

Magda There's nothing here we haven't done a hundred times before.

Miles There could be with development.

Magda There could be if we make it up.

Miles You're such a fucking purist! This is raw material! First drafts begging to be rewritten! We make them work. We make them real. So real they'll believe it themselves. And they love what they see!

Come back with me. I can't live like this any more.

Pause.

Magda I have never been so happy.

Enter Peter from the office.

I told you to wait inside!

Enter Lynette from the other direction. She rather clearly has no bra on.

Lynette Hello.

Miles Hello.

Lynette Lynette Seal. Dancer. Hostess. Dinner partner. I'm here to turn a B minus into an A double plus.

Miles Miles Trafford.

Lynette Producer.

Miles Yes. Nice to meet you, Lynette.

Lynette Would you like to hear my unique selling point?

Miles Excuse me?

Lynette Well, Miles, there I was in the youth club with Michelle and Sarah and we were just saying how all the boys were such stiffs and not worth our time? When this man comes in and on first glance I just know that he's special.

Miles Lynette. Forgive my bluntness. What are you talking about?

Lynette Oh. Well, basically, I've got one tit with a silicon implant and one without. This is the one with.

She points to the one. Pause.

Miles That's . . . that's . . .

Lynette Listen, Miles, if it's tragedy you're after, don't look at me. This one's just knifed his father to death.

Blackout.

SCENE TWO

8.00 p.m. A small living-room in an old railwayman's cottage. An opening leading to a small hall. The front door is visible. The hall leads to some unseen stairs going up. In the living-room, a doorway leading to a small kitchen. A window in the front wall. A window in the back. The curtains are closed.

The living room has a sofa, a separate armchair, sideboards and a large cupboard which is closed.

The place is in total disarray. Beer bottles, whisky bottles, and other spirits lie around the floor. Old plates with pizzas have been left in various areas of the room. Cobwebs on the ceilings. On one of the walls there are old bones hung from string. A lot of the furniture is knocked over. The place is dark, old raggedy curtains hiding the light. An upside-down crucifix on the wall. No lampshade on the bulb. The kitchen we can just about see is a total tip.

On the table in front of the sofa is a knife covered in blood. There is blood smeared on the walls. Blood on the carpet.

Tiffany sits on the sofa. She stares at the knife. Then she goes over to the front door, turns to face the room. She faints. She stands. Faints again.

She hears a noise. A car approaching. Headlights in the night. She immediately goes to the window and flies out into the night, closing the window behind her.

A train rattles past, shaking the walls of the house. Enter Peter, Magda, and Miles through the front door. They enter the living-room.

Peter Sorry about the mess. I didn't have time to tidy.

Peter heads through the room and into the kitchen. Miles and Magda stare at the débâcle.
Peter returns, bemused, a bit embarrassed.

He's disappeared.

Pause.

Magda Disappeared?

Peter He was lying here. I don't know where he's gone.

Miles I thought you killed him.

Peter I thought I did.

Pause.

I'm cutting veg, for tea. He's in a rage. He stands there, massive in the doorway, staring at me. I'm like, 'Say something. Dad, if you're angry, scream, shout, just say something.' He stands there. I can't take it, his eyes in my back. I turn to confront him, have it out once and for all. He must have moved forward, he's so quiet when he moves. It goes in. Sticking in his chest like a cake.

Miles And then?

Peter Then I ran.

Magda I'll look upstairs.

Peter No, I'll go. Let me go.

Peter dashes upstairs. Miles picks up the knife.

Miles Magda, is there something you haven't told me?

Magda dials on her mobile phone.

Magda Is that Accident and Emergency? Well could you put me through. Is that A and E? Has a Roger Watson been to you in the last hour? Well, could you look please? (*Beat.*) Yes, this is Magda. Who's this? Oh, hello. Yes, I remember you. Double joints, yes. Yes, I'm keeping you on file, would you look please, it's rather urgent. No one of that name. You're sure? Thank you. Thank you! (*She hangs up.*)

Pause.

Magda It's just a story.

Miles So was *Hamlet*. Some catch on.

Magda It's something I've been working on. I wasn't even sure if it would come to anything.

Miles That fear would appear to be unfounded.

Pause.

Magda All right. I decide if this goes in. Not you. Not Danny.

Miles Absolutely.

Magda I've been working on this for two months. All the others were just cover for what I was really up to. What is really happening here.

Miles Which is?

Pause.

Magda It was my third day at the church. I was at a real low. People were arriving in their droves. Queuing all through the sacristy. They were so fucking eager. It's not as if they had anything to offer. Just drunkards and doomed love triangles.

Miles God save us.

Magda I was thinking of giving it all up. Coming home. It was nearly midnight. Everyone had gone. This boy shuffled in. Pale face. Big black coat, wouldn't take it off, wouldn't sit down, wouldn't look at me. He barely spoke. Then he left. But his eyes. Such sadness. He had to be hiding something.

Miles He came back . . .

Magda Three days later. The same pale face. The same coat. He was so still. Then he spoke. His mother is dead. His father is a monster in whose shadow he lives in pure terror.

Miles Classic grief-fuelled tyranny. Where's the twist?

Beat.

Magda I begged him to come back. He didn't. A week passed. More drunkards. More men with hair loss. I was desperate. Then Tiffany came.

Miles New character . . .

Magda Peter's younger sister. She knocked on the door early one morning. She was terrified. She made me swear not to tell Peter. In ten minutes I knew everything.

Miles Yes? What?

Magda The mother killed herself. The family covered it up between them. They made it look like an accident.

Beat.

Miles OK, now we're cooking with gas. Why did she do it?

Magda I imagine life didn't grab her.

Miles Violence?

Magda Days of silence. Nights of drunken terror, all hushed up the next morning. The father has a fascination with the dead that infects his family like a virus.

Miles Oh, that is actually very beautiful.

Magda He works in burials. Digs the graves. Fills them in after. When she died . . .

Miles Yes?

Magda He buried her himself.

Miles Oh my.

Magda He visits her grave every day . . .

Miles Oh my.

Magda . . . then comes back home and punishes his kids.

Miles How?

Magda He makes them perform rituals. He brings back old bones he's dug up while preparing graves. Hangs them on the wall.

Pause.

They offer satanic chants. They do ouija. They try to raise the dead. The father believes that the mother's spirit has escaped the grave. It's sunk several feet since the burial. Apparently that's the sign.

Miles Who else knows about this?

Magda They tend to keep themselves to themselves. He's taken them out of school. They have no friends. No family. No one in the town has any idea this is happening. No one even knows we meet. Peter makes me swear to keep it that way. He's not even in the file. That's how scared they are. Then this week he suddenly announces he wants to go on the show. I ask why. 'I want the world to know what is happening in my house.'

Miles If this isn't underbelly, I would like to know what is.

Magda Notice something strange about the room? Think. You walk into a church and the altar's missing.

Miles Where's the . . . ? (*Beat.*) You don't mean? But they have to.

Magda They don't.

Miles But they have to.

Magda He told them it's the devil talking.

Miles He what?

Magda They have never seen *The Danny Crowe Show.*

Miles No no no.

Magda They had never even heard of *The Danny Crowe Show.*

Miles But that just doesn't happen. I mean *everyone*'s heard of *The Danny Crowe Show*!

Magda Look around you. No television. No radio. No music. No magazines. No phone.

Miles No phone?

Magda They're savages, Miles. Everything they do is based on the most simple instincts of terror and need. They have no concept of money or fame or success. They just survive, day to day, breath to breath. It's as they're if untouched by human hand. And I found them.

Peter comes down.

Peter He's not there. I'm checking outside.

Pause.

Magda Are you all right?

Peter Yeah.

Magda Do you want me to come with you?

Peter Yeah.

They leave through the front door. Miles checks the window and calls on his phone.

Miles Danny? Danny, it's Miles. Listen, something unbelievable has happened. You're not going to believe who I have found! (*Beat.*) Danny, why are shouting? Danny, will you listen to me. I have found . . . . Danny stop swearing at me. I said stop swearing! No, I didn't get your message. I turned it off. I'm trying to explain why! Something unbelievable is happening here! (*Beat.*) What about the live special? What about the obese twins? I thought you loved the obese twins. (*Pause.*) They're not obese? What do you mean they're not obese? They're not twins? They're actresses? (*Shouts a raging fuck away from the phone.*) OK Danny, listen. I had no idea they were actresses. (*Beat.*) OK, I knew they were actresses. Yes, I faked them. Yes, I padded them. Danny, you have no idea how much pressure I have been under! I have been doing three shows a week minimum, Danny, and I just don't have time to find the material! This was the live special! You were so fucking desperate for underbelly and I hadn't come up trumps! I know we can't use them! I know we're screwed! Danny, you're chanting. Why are you chanting? Where are you? A weekend retreat in Brittany? What kind of retreat? . . . Since when were you Buddhist? . . . (*Beat.*)

Danny, you don't mean that. I don't think you mean that Danny, you're just upset. Danny, you can't fire me. How long have I worked for you? This is my whole life, this is what I do. Danny, listen! Danny, that is not real chanting! You're only chanting so you don't have to listen! . . . I know you're in the shitter! I know you have two days to find another show!

Pause.

Danny. I have found you another show. I said I have found you another show. That's what I was calling you about. Yes! I was feeling guilty about the actresses and I decided to go out and find you another show! No, this is really something Danny. It's Swedenborg meets Sam Raimi . . . The details aren't a hundred per cent clear to me, but I can tell you it's a gothic domestic tragedy, very real, very dark. Blood on the carpet. Bones on the walls. And it ends with a son stabbing his father. Oh yes. Now listen. I know I've been off form these last few months . . . I don't know what happened, for some crazy reason I've been losing the will to live. But I am dealing with that. I am dealing with everything! Who knows about the twins? Just you me and Henrietta? OK tell Henrietta to keep her equine trap shut, tell her to dump the twins, and no one need know this ever happened. And if by Monday morning I haven't supplied you with the rawest slice of underbelly you have ever tasted, then please fire me. Throw me on the slag heap of history. But come on, Danny. Give me one more chance, Danny. Buddha would. . . . Thank you. Thank you. Thank you.

Magda enters. Miles sees her and changes his tone to extremely casual.

Listen, I'll call you later. Yup. (*He hangs up.*)

Magda Who was that?

Miles No one.

Magda It's OK, you can say.

Miles Say what?

Magda Miles, I mean it's fine, but I know that look. That was a woman.

Miles (*beat*) Yes. Yes, it was.

Magda I know.

Miles She's just a friend.

Magda I knew it.

Miles Nothing serious.

Magda It's fine. What's her name?

Miles Her name is Danielle.

Magda So you've moved on.

Miles I can honestly say we haven't done anything.

Magda But you're seeing her. Tell me, really.

Miles Well, what did you expect me to do, go into mourning, alone in my room, not seeing anyone for weeks, spiralling into despair and misery, ruining my life in an act of wilful self-destruction?

Magda Is she pretty?

Miles Stunning. Any sign of the corpse?

Magda He's not dead. Peter must have panicked. No. (*to the window*) He's out there somewhere. Waiting. (*Pause.*) The hours I've spent imagining what this room looked like. You never get it right.

Miles So. What do we do now?

Magda I have to meet the father.

Miles You've never met him?

Magda He has no idea Peter's been coming to me. I want him, Miles. I want him on the show.

Miles Is that likely?

Magda I asked Peter. He said he'd arrange it. That was the last time we met.

Peter returns from outside, shutting the door behind him.

Peter He's gone.

Magda Would he call someone, Peter?

Peter He doesn't call anyone.

Magda Where would he go? Think, anything at all that could help us.

Peter Maybe the cemetery. He likes to go walking there alone.

Magda Why was he angry with you? Try and tell us, Peter.

Peter I asked him. If he would meet you. I told him about you. That's why he was mad. He said he'd kill me, and you, and anyone that knew.

They stare at each other. Pause. Suddenly the sound of a key struggling with front door lock. They freeze.

Miles Is there a back way out?

Peter You can try the window.

Miles Come on. (*Beat.*) What are you waiting for?

Magda Don't you want to talk to him, Miles?

Miles You see him as a conversationalist?

Magda But don't you just have to meet him?

The door opens. It is Tiffany. She is pale. Her hands are covered with blood. She holds out her father's keys and speaks quietly.

Peter Tiffany?

Tiffany (*a whisper*) Dad. In the cemetery. Shoulder carved open. Bare nerves. Tried to stem the flow. He won't come back. Wants to stay there . . . with the graves and the tombs . . . Says he'll kill you if he sees you . . .

Tiffany faints. Peter runs to her. Magda runs to get her coat.

Magda Where is he? (*to Tiffany*) Where is he, Tiffany?

Tiffany (*a whisper*) Walk along the tracks, you come to the cemetery gates. He's in on the left. Near Basil Ramsay. Died 1934.

Magda (*to Peter*) I'm leaving my phone. Call this number if anything happens. (*to Tiffany*) Give me your keys.

Miles What are you doing?

Magda I'm going to convince him he should come on the show.

Miles Are you insane?

Magda Are you coming?

Magda leaves. Miles grabs his coat and follows. They leave and close the door. Oddly long pause. Peter checks the window. When he speaks it is with a completely different air, confident and sharp.

Peter You were seven seconds late.

Tiffany Sorry. I was putting some blood on my hands. (*Produces a bottle.*)

Peter What is it?

Tiffany Bull's blood it's called. It's not really bull's blood. That's what they call it.

Peter Does it come off carpets?

Tiffany It does.

> *She leaps up and runs into the kitchen with the bottle of blood. Tiffany washes her hands in the kitchen.*

Tiffany Who's the guy with her?

Peter Miles Trafford. Producer and ex-lover.

> *Tiffany returns.*

Tiffany That's monger Miles? No wonder she left him. (*Tiffany takes out some Mintoes and eats two.*) How did it go?

Peter It was if I may say so the best yet.

Tiffany Go on, then.

Peter (*to Tiffany but with exactly the same reality as before*) I'm cutting veg for tea. He's in a rage. He stands there. I can't take it, his eyes in my back. I turn to confront him, have it out once and for all. He must have moved forward, he's so quiet when he moves. It goes in. Sticking in his chest like it's a cake.

Tiffany (*moved*) What did she think?

Peter She loved it of course.

Tiffany Too right. Gets you right there that does. (*She faints.*)

Peter Your hand stopped your fall.

Tiffany (*leaping up*) It did not!

Peter Say it with me, Tiffany.

Peter/Tiffany Realism! Realism! Realism!

Peter You know why he's here, don't you? He's giving us the nod.

Tiffany You mean . . . ?

Peter She wants us and Trafford's here to give producer's approval.

Tiffany Oh my God.

Peter Of course we still need to surmount the tricky issue of her wanting the father.

Tiffany Which we're doing now . . .

Peter Which we're doing now . . . And once that's achieved we shall be on our way.

Tiffany The big trip out of here.

Peter To London.

Tiffany To Danny Crowe.

Peter/Tiffany The Pope of Pain!

Peter presses some buttons on Magda's phone

Tiffany What you doing?

Peter She might have Danny's number on here.

Tiffany Oh my God.

Peter (*shows Tiffany*) Home and mobile.

Tiffany Oh my God! Let's call him.

Peter What if he answers?

Tiffany We don't have to say anything. We could just listen to him saying hello.

Peter He'll do 1471.

Tiffany You can nix that.

Peter All right. I'm dialling his home. (*Peter dials. Pause. Peter hangs up.*)

Tiffany What did he say? What did he say?

Peter This is Danny Crowe I'm not in leave a message after the tone.

Pause.

Tiffany What are you thinking about?

Peter I'm thinking about sitting on the sofa.

Tiffany I knew you were.

Peter He's there, microphone in his hand, his face sober and serious, his brow glistening with compassion. The audience hush. The cameras roll. He takes a step forward, and fixes me with that deep and penetrating gaze. (*being Danny, using a beer bottle as a mike*) Peter, it will really help you if you can talk. You may find it a deeply healing experience. Can you try? Can you? (*as his character to Danny, very real*) Thing is Danny, my mother was fragile, like cut glass . . . (*as Danny*) Did you try to help her, give her the support she needed? (*to Danny*) Of course I did. But he was always in the way, this black hole sucking us deeper, ever deeper into the darkness until there was no way out. (*as Danny*) And physically such a large man. Wild, violent. That must have wounded you, deeply? (*to Danny, whispered pain*) Yeah. (*as Danny*) And no mother to offer relief, the love only a mother can give. (*to Danny, suddenly saddened*) There's not a day goes by when I don't see her face. She had the most beautiful face. Little freckles on her cheeks like a kid. And when she smiled, it was the smile of an angel.

Tiffany That was great, that last bit.

Peter Not too mawkish?

Tiffany No way!

Peter I despise mawkishness.

Tiffany Anyway, she did have a lovely face.

Pause.

Peter Who did?

Tiffany Your mum.

Peter What's my mother got to do with it?

Tiffany Nothing. I just mean . . .

Peter I'm not talking about *my* mother. I'm talking about *the* mother.

Tiffany Right.

Peter There's no resemblance between *my* mother and *the* mother.

Tiffany Your mum did have freckles.

Peter That is a coincidence, a complete and baffling coincidence. The mother in this story is quite a lot taller than my mother, and a whole lot paler and more serene.

Tiffany Oh, right.

Peter My mother! Besides the fact that I only have the haziest memory of what she looked like anyway, you think Danny Crowe wants a bog standard workaday mother? The mother in this story is nothing like that! She's a paragon! A goddess threatened by demonic powers! She's much more of a Meryl Streep figure.

Tiffany And she has a daughter. That was a brilliant touch of yours.

Peter (*taking out a spray can of cobwebs and touching up the walls*) Double the victims, double the sympathy. Also more believable that the daughter tells a slightly different side to the story. Also, they like to have two people on the sofa. The daughter was just begging to be introduced.

Tiffany Why did you choose me to play her?

Peter Well, firstly you were available. And secondly you have a dynamic, haunted quality.

Tiffany Do I really? (*She tries to look dynamic, haunted.*) Do you think your dad'll mind being called a murderer on national television?

Peter By the time he finds out I'll be cutting my first single.

Tiffany I'm doing backing!

Peter Then it's straight on to the circuit. Presenting at the Brits, having a gas with Graham Norton, playing football in Uganda for Comic Relief, and then across the pond to sell the movie rights.

Tiffany Who'll play me?

Peter Julia Stiles is my choice.

Tiffany I see myself more as Anna Friel.

Peter But can she do an American accent?

Tiffany They all can these days. What about you?

Peter Tobey Maguire. Or if Tobey's deep in Batman, Ethan Hawke. And the father'll be Ed Harris. With a scar. He'll win a Best Supporting Actor because they like to give it to the older man.

Tiffany When's he back?

Peter Ed Harris?

Tiffany Your dad.

Peter Oh. (*Peter stops spraying.*) Tomorrow morning. He's staying at a motel. It's a crematorium staff awayday.

Tiffany He's always doing them.

Peter It's for morale. They play squash and discuss cremation procedure.

   Pause.

Tiffany He's going to miss you.

Peter Do you think so? (*Beat.*) I don't think so.

Tiffany Since she left him, you're pretty much all he's got.

Peter He's got the other ushers at the crematorium.

Tiffany I don't think they provide much consolation.

Peter Yeah, well. He forgot her. He'll forget me soon enough.

Tiffany How do you know he's forgotten her?

Peter When does he even mention her? My father doesn't need the company of living people. Dead ones suit him fine.

   The mobile phone rings. Peter picks it up. He changes his tone back to the hushed rural Cheshire accent of before.

Peter Hello. He's not there? (*as if to Tiffany*) He's not there. There's some blood? Really? You're coming back? OK. (*He puts the phone down.*)

Tiffany Oh my God.

Peter Right. This is your big scene, Tiffany. Are you ready for this?

Tiffany I think so.

Peter Think so's not good enough, Tiffany. I spent all yesterday writing this and I cannot afford think so!

Tiffany I'm ready, Peter.

Peter Look at me. (*Beat.*) Why do they love us?

Tiffany Because our pain is great!

Peter Why do they want us?!

Tiffany Because our need is real!

The key struggles in the lock. Tiffany immediately goes to the sofa, Peter to the back window.

Peter Tiff.

Tiffany Yeah.

Peter You're my best friend in the world.

Tiffany I'm your only friend.

Peter That still makes you my best.

Peter leaves through the back window. Tiffany suddenly speaks to a fictional camera. It is oddly real.

Tiffany Basically, Danny, Peter is a special person, and very misunderstood. I feel I am the only woman who has ever really got close to him. I know the strange workings of his heart . . . Yes, Danny, I suppose you could call that a certain kind of love.

She leaps back on to the sofa in a post-swoon posture. The key opens the door. Enter Magda and Miles.

Magda Where's Peter?

Tiffany (*whispers*) I told him not to. I told him it was dangerous. But he wouldn't listen!

Magda Where is he?

Tiffany He's gone to lay flowers on mother's grave. He does it every day at this time. I normally go with him, to sing songs and weep, but what with my dizzy spell . . . I begged him not to. Dad'll know where to find him.

Magda Where is it? I'll go to him.

Tiffany No! Family rule number one. Nobody is allowed to the grave except us. We just have to wait. Wait and hope.

Miles (*to Magda*) I think we should go with what we've got.

Magda I will decide when I go.

Miles I'm just saying it's already definitively underbelly, that's all I'm saying.

Tiffany (*to Magda*) I don't know how to say this. I really don't. You've been so good to us. You're a saint, Magda. You headed out into the jungle with your Bible and your scythe and you found us, the forgotten people! You found us and you cured our pain. Our very great pain. Our very real need. Every night Peter comes into my bedroom and tells me about you, about your eyes, the eyes of a saviour. But you can't let us down now! We've gone too far. We can't go back.

Magda I won't let you down.

Tiffany I don't even want to think about it. Swiss rolls, Wagon Wheels, entire tin assortments emptied in a morning . . . I just . . . I hated myself. I filled my cave of a heart with caramel. It's in my nature, once I start something I have to see it through, until it takes me down a spiral, a vortex of loathing . . .

Pause.

If it hadn't been for Peter. He brought me out of it. He was so kind, so patient. And to think of him all alone at the burial site. It breaks my heart. The bitter irony that that man we call our father, that heavy devil, still stands between us and our freedom. Because you know what? He won't go, Magda. Hand on my heart. My father is not the talk-show type.

The front door opens. Enter Peter.

Tiffany What is it?

Peter I just met him at the grave.

Tiffany Oh my God.

Peter He came up out of the darkness. He was all bandaged up. He'd been drinking. His eyes were burning orange fire. I thought, he's going to kill me. He looked at me and smiled. He said 'Peter I'm going out on an insane bender for the night and if I find you in my house when I get back tomorrow morning, it'll be your bones that are hung on our living room wall.' Then he laughed and heaved his giant frame back into the forest whence he came.

Pause.

Magda I worked so hard for this.

Miles It's still the show of the year.

Magda I wanted more than that!

Miles You may have to wait for the sequel.

Pause.

Magda OK. I have to clear up at the church. Get packed. Take enough clothes for three days.

Tiffany What do you mean?

Miles She means you're going to Danny Crowe.

Tiffany Oh my God.

Miles Well done, Magda. We're going to knock them dead with this one.

Pause.

Magda That's twice now you've said we.

Miles Well, I just thought it would be fitting if we took it together.

Magda Fitting?

Miles Think of it as a symbol. We walk into that studio bearing the fruit of our labour before us.

Magda Our labour?

Miles I have double-shifted for you for four months.

Magda I didn't ask you to do that.

Miles Without me you wouldn't even have a job. Danny doesn't take kindly to people wandering off into the unknown. Now if we take this together, I think I can swing it. I'll say that we've been developing it in secret because it was delicate. We don't need to mention the mill-towns or the tending to the two thousand . . .

Magda Why do you need a show?

Miles I don't.

Magda You have a live special on Monday.

Miles You know what I'm going to do? I'm going to dump the obese twins. I mean they were great, but sacrifices have to be made. I'm going to make this the live special.

Magda You have no right to do that.

Miles Think of it as my gesture to you. A way of saying that what's past is past!

Magda I can't accept it.

Miles Why must you always make things so unbelievably difficult?

Magda I can't do it with you.

Miles Listen, I'll take second billing. I just want to be able to say that I was involved! That's all I need! Can't you even give me that!

Magda I can't go back to how we were.

Pause.

Miles What do you mean?

Magda I can't go back to living with you.

Miles You want to find your own place for a while?

Magda I can't go back to being with you.

Miles You mean . . . You don't mean . . .

Magda I don't know what I'm going to do. I may find a place of my own. I may come back up here. I just can't be near you.

Pause.

Miles Right.

Magda I'm sorry.

Miles No, fine. I mean it was only seven years . . .

Magda I really am.

Miles And best to do it in public.

Magda I didn't intend this.

Pause.

Miles No, that's fine. I mean if that's the way you want to play it.

Magda What does that mean?

Miles Nothing. I'll tell Danny you're bringing it on your own. Save you a call.

Magda Miles, listen.

Miles Is there anything else we have to discuss?

Magda I don't know.

Miles Do you have anything to say?

Magda I don't know, Miles!

Miles Nor do I. So. Why don't you give me a lift to my car? (*Exit Miles.*)

Magda Don't go out. Don't answer the door. I'll be back in two hours to pick you up.

Exit Magda. Peter clutches his chest.

Peter Tiffany. Please tell me what you think she just said.

Tiffany I think she just said we're going to Danny Crowe.

Peter That's what I heard.

Tiffany Oh, Peter.

Peter There's no air in here.

Tiffany Oh, Peter!

Peter I need oxygen.

Tiffany Where's your thingy?

Peter In the basket.

Tiffany fetches an inhaler. Peter inhales.

Tiffany Oh, Peter! Oh, Peter!

A ring at the door. Peter hides the inhaler back in the basket. Tiffany goes to answer it. It is Miles.

Tiffany Hello, Miles.

Miles (*rather loudly*) Can I use your bathroom?

Tiffany Of course. Don't mind us, we're just trying to let it all slowly sink in.

Miles enters. Pause. Peter indicates through the kitchen.

Peter It's through there.

Miles What is?

Peter The bathroom.

Miles Oh.

Pause.

OK, let me explain. Magda has been here for four months. The fact is she was fired three months ago, but I have been doing her work for her in the absurd belief that she would return. Without me, that bitch has no job to go back to. She cannot guarantee you a show. She cannot guarantee you anything. I do have a job, and I also have a live special on Monday which is begging to be filled. I am going to get my car and come back, and if I don't prove that what I have told you is true, then tell me to get screwed and go with her. But if I do prove it, and I will, then you'd be wise to go with me. It's commonly known as a no-lose situation and you'd be fools to refuse it. Agreed?

They nod.

Good. See you in an hour.

Miles undoes his fly and then makes a good act of doing it up again as he leaves through the front door. Tiffany and Peter look at each other.
   Blackout.

SCENE THREE

Tiffany is trying on a frock and putting on make-up. It is a few minutes before ten. Bags are all over the floor. It is raining hard outside.

Tiffany This dress, Ulrika? This was given me by Donatella Versace. I holiday on her yacht when my schedule allows. Yes, the one featured in *Hello* magazine. 'How My Yacht Helped Me Get Over Gianni.' You're right of course, my tough working-class background does make me more aware of the crazy injustice of it all. Sometimes I sit here in my rangy country abode, conveniently located within easy reach of the metropolis and with the Beckhams and Kriss Akabusi as close neighbours, and I think: so much hunger in the world, so much poverty, does a luxury Scandinavian kitchen really matter?

   Enter Peter with a small holdall as Tiffany continues to pack her nine bags.

Peter Are you sure you've got enough luggage there Tiffany?

Tiffany Do you think I've overdone it?

Peter What's in them?

Tiffany Clothes, make-up, personal accessories, magazines, spiritual awakening Bible, mementoes of previous life, hairspray, Dougray the bear, Mintoes, and underwear. Oh, and that one's got a photograph of Mum to put on my mansion wall.

The sound of a phone ringing from inside a cupboard.

Peter Fucking hell, Tiffany. Didn't you disconnect it?

Tiffany I thought I did.

Peter It could have rung when they were here!

Tiffany Well it didn't did it? (*Tiffany opens the cupboard and picks up the cordless phone.*) Hello? (*to Peter*) It's Pizza Pronto. They want to know if you're free to do deliveries tomorrow.

Peter (*takes phone*) Who's that? Ahmed? No, can you tell Billy I'm not free tomorrow. Tell him I'll be installed in the safe house of a national television show. Yeah. All right then. (*He puts the phone down, disconnecting it, and closes the cupboard.*)

Tiffany Just think, Peter. You'll never have to deliver pizza again.

Peter I might. I might become a celebrity millionaire and suddenly have a yen to deliver pizzas to other celebrity millionaires in my Maserati. I rule nothing out.

Tiffany If you could deliver pizza to anyone in the world, who would it be?

Peter Nelson Mandela. And then Kylie.

Tiffany She's not allowed pizza. It's not in her regime.

Peter She can have Salad Nicoise.

Tiffany My mum is going to sit down on Monday evening, turn on the telly, and see me on the purple sofa. She'll have a fucking heart attack.

Peter I think you'll find we discussed that, Tiffany.

Tiffany I know.

Peter And what did we conclude?

Tiffany I'll write to her after. She can come visit me in Primrose Hill and I'll buy her a mocchacino.

Pause.

Peter What?

Tiffany Nothing. I just thought.

Peter What?

Tiffany Your mum might watch it.

Pause.

Peter What do you mean?

Tiffany Well she might, mightn't she? I mean she always used to watch it.

Peter Just because she used to watch it doesn't mean she'll watch it now.

Tiffany You don't know that though, do you? You don't even know where she is. For all you know, she might be sitting in her new home having a cup of tea and there right in front of her is the son she left five years ago without so much as a goodbye.

Peter She left a letter.

Tiffany Oh well, that's all right then.

Peter She left a letter saying she needed some time to find her inner self.

Tiffany It must be fucking well-hidden.

Peter I don't know why you keep harping on about her. As far as I'm concerned my mother is history.

Tiffany All right.

Peter I'm seriously thinking of not including her in my autobiography.

Pause.

And if I do it will only be because the market demands it.

Pause.

I mean, if it means books are flying off the shelves . . . then who am I to say otherwise . . . but apart from that . . . she's on the cutting-room floor.

Tiffany Is something wrong, Peter? Are you having second thoughts?

Peter I don't want him taking us.

Tiffany Why not?

Peter She found us. She should take us.

Tiffany What difference does it make who takes us?

Peter She understands us. He's just a huckster.

Pause.

Tiffany Do you like her?

Peter Of course I don't.

Tiffany I'll fucking kill you if you like her.

Peter She's over thirty, Tiffany.

Tiffany All you ever do is talk about her. Her natural empathy. Her capacity for understanding a person's pain.

Peter She's invested a lot of personal energy in this story.

Tiffany If she likes you that's her funeral. I'm just saying you better not fucking like her.

Peter You know perfectly well my position on love.

Tiffany It's an investment of time and energy that the ambitious modern man cannot afford.

Peter Thank you very much.

Tiffany Then why the palaver?

Peter I don't like leading people on.

Tiffany Yeah, well, maybe you should have thought of that three months ago.

The bell rings. Pause.

Peter Tiffany. Looks like we're not in Kansas any more.

Peter and Tiffany go to the door and open. Roger enters. A small man, balding, soaked wet.

Roger Sorry, I couldn't find my key and it's cats and dogs out there.

Pause as Roger sees the house.

Peter What are you doing here?

Roger It's my house.

Peter But what happened to the crematorium awayday?

Roger It finished early.

Peter They never finish early.

Roger Well, this one did.

Peter Didn't you play squash?

Roger We did a bit.

Peter Well, couldn't you go back and play some more?

Roger What's in God's name is going on here?

Peter What do you mean, what's going on? I should be the one asking you!

Pause.

Oh you mean . . .

Roger I mean the carnage in my living-room!

Pause.

Why is there blood on the carpet?

Tiffany It's not real blood. It's bull's blood.

Peter It's not really bull's blood. That's what they call it.

Tiffany It's from a bottle.

Peter It comes off. Show him, Tiffany.

Roger I don't care if it comes off, I want to know how it got on. This place was spick and span when I left here this morning.

Pause.

Roger Where's the telly?

Peter It's . . . it's . . .

Roger What have you done with the telly? You'd better not have broken it, it's brand new that is. I only splashed out because you made such a song and dance about it. (*Pause. Roger sees the bones.*) What in God's name are they?

Peter Sheep's bones. They're from the butchers.

Roger What are they doing on my wall? Well, I'm waiting.

Pause.

Tiffany We might as well tell him the truth, Peter.

Peter What?

Tiffany The fact is, Mr Watson, that we took advantage of your absence to organise a wild fancy-dress party with a horror movie theme.

Roger Is that right? Well I appreciate your honesty, Tiffany.

Tiffany I hope you won't hold it against us, Mr Watson, we're just a couple of teenagers making the mistakes teenagers make.

Roger Where are your guests?

Peter They've gone.

Roger It's five past ten.

Peter Yes, it finished at ten. It was pretty full on while it lasted, but people have lives to lead.

Roger It's Saturday night.

Peter We've learned from the mistakes of previous generations. We know when to say: enough's enough.

Tiffany Which also explains why we chose to hide the telly in the cupboard lest it be damaged by an overly zestful dancer.

Roger Is that why you're wearing that ridiculous get-up?

Peter Yeah. I'm the dark one from *Blair Witch* and Tiffany's from *Halloween Three*.

Roger And it's over?

Peter Yeah.

Tiffany It's not my place to tell you what to do, Mr Watson, but if you were to decide to turn in, then we could clear up and by morning all this will seem like nothing more than a bad dream.

Pause.

Mr Watson?

Roger Have you held parties before, when I go away?

Pause.

Peter Yeah, loads.

Roger I never noticed.

Peter Really? Oh, they were pretty wild.

Roger It was as if no one had ever crossed the threshold.

Peter Yeah, well I did my best not to upset you.

Pause.

Tiffany Is there something wrong, Mr Watson?

Peter Dad?

Roger Do you feel you have to wait for me to go away to enjoy yourself?

Peter What?

Roger All this time, doing everything behind my back. You could have asked me. I wouldn't have minded.

Peter I'll consider that for next time, shall I?

Roger I worry about you. Staying in all day. I don't want to deny you fun. I don't mean to.

Peter Why don't we talk about it in the morning?

Roger Why can't we talk about it now?

Peter We've waited sixteen years to have a conversation, I just thought we could hang on another night.

Pause.

Dad?

Roger I'm sorry. Ridiculous. I don't know what's come over me.

He starts to shake. Peter seems quite unable to help him.

Peter What is it?

Roger Peter. Would you hold me please?

Peter Why?

Roger I don't know. I really just don't know. Tiffany, I can tell you I'm really not like this. (*Beat.*) I'm not like this. (*He gestures.*)

Peter What?

Roger Hold me, Peter. Please.

Peter Dad, don't take it personally. It's just we don't hold. It's not something we do.

Roger You're my son.

Peter I know, but there are limits.

Roger Peter, help me. I'm going mad here, son.

Peter approaches and they air-hug with terrible awkwardness.

Peter Right, that's that done. Listen, you must be all in. We'll clear up.

Roger I need to speak to you.

Peter We just have. I mean I really enjoyed it.

Roger Tiffany, will you be wanting a lift home?

Tiffany Am I leaving?

Roger I have to speak to my son.

Peter Well, you can't. I'm a very busy man, I can't just be having conversations!

Roger Peter.

Peter If you must talk to someone, there's got to be another awayday you can go on. Or there are helplines – Samaritans – a problem shared is a problem halved. I'll get you a number if you like.

Roger I don't want to talk to anyone. I want to talk to you. Now I am taking my bag upstairs and then I am driving Tiffany home. And I'd appreciate it if you clear up while I'm gone. (*Roger exits upstairs.*)

Pause.

Tiffany What do we do now?

Peter We continue with our typical clarity of focus and positive attitude.

Tiffany Yeah, but he's taking me home.

Peter No he's not.

Tiffany It's all over if he takes me home.

Peter He's not.

Tiffany No show. No Moccachino. No mansion. No movie.

Peter He won't take you home, Tiffany, I've got it all worked out.

Tiffany Ed Harris can kiss goodbye to that Oscar.

Peter Tiffany, I am dealing with the situation!

Tiffany I don't know.

Peter What?

Tiffany I mean when do crematoria awaydays ever finish early?

Peter What are you saying?

Tiffany Fate, Peter. Destiny. I know we've both worked so hard for this, two months of writing and rewriting, hours of rehearsing, fine-tuning script and performance to an unrivalled level of professionalism, but sometimes you just have to say . . .

Peter What?

Tiffany If only we'd got on *Survivor* or *Mole* or *Big Brother* . . .

Peter What are you saying, Tiffany?

Tiffany I'm saying maybe we're not destined for TV stardom.

Beat.

Peter Say that again. Say that . . .

Tiffany Not everyone can rise, Peter. If they did, there wouldn't be anywhere to rise from, and then where we would we be?

Peter Now you listen to me. You eliminate that negative thinking right now! You may be an actress with a peculiarly dramatic haunted quality, Tiffany. But that quality is worth *nothing* unless it is allied with a mental toughness and a finisher's poise. An ability to stay focused. An ability to maintain sight of our goals whatever the pressure.

Tiffany I can't help it if I have feelings.

Peter And you think I don't? You think I don't have emotions that well up in me like a wave threatening to drown everything in a torrent? The achievement of true celebrity requires discipline! We have to batten down the hatches! We have to stand guard against the tiniest hole! If we could actually do something, sing, dance, play golf, then it would be different. We could afford to relax confident in the knowledge that our natural ability would see us through. But we haven't got any ability!

Tiffany You said ability is irrelevant in the acquisition of true fame. You said, 'Look at the list of celebrity millionaires who don't have ability.'

Peter And you think they let an obstacle like this stand between them and their ambition? This is the modern world, you get one shot and if you are one of the few to take it, it rewards you, with great riches, and friends, and lovers, and pools, and all the joys of the celebrity lifestyle. But if you miss it, it haunts you for the rest of your life. I won't be stuck here with that sad bastard stirring tea in ever slower circles, meandering into meaninglessness and anonymity. Staring at soggy pizza, watching other people rise, and thinking of what might have been. I am worth more than that! I have ideas. I have dreams! What am I going to do with them stuck here? Write them on fucking calzones?

Pause.

There is no greater threat to our enterprise, Tiffany, than the frailty of the human heart.

Roger returns down the stairs.

Roger You all set, Tiffany?

Peter You're not taking her, Dad.

Roger Why not?

Peter Because. Because . . . because . . . tell him, Tiffany.

Pause.

Tiffany If I can explain, Mr Watson. Peter and I were having a post-party soirée together. We were hoping we could spend a bit of time alone.

Roger You can see each other every day.

Tiffany But intimately. *A deux*.

Roger You don't mean . . . romantically?

Tiffany nods. She takes Peter by the hand.

But you two are friends. Peter likes you Tiffany, but nothing more. He's always been extremely clear about that.

Tiffany Has he? Well, things change, Mr Watson. Peter has tonight delved into the secret chamber of his heart and discovered that he is actually very much in love with me. He told me so just before you arrived.

Roger And do you feel the same way?

Tiffany We were hoping to watch *Sleepless in Seattle* together, in each other's arms.

Roger Why didn't you say so Peter?

Peter . . .

Tiffany He wasn't sure what you'd think.

Roger What do you mean? Have you any idea how worried about you I've been? Never leaving the house. Not getting dressed for days at a time. Eating leftovers from undelivered pizza. Drinking flat coke. If you're not watching that damn box for hours on end, your head's stuck in those magazines like they're the bloody Bible. Take away Tiffany, I didn't think you had friends at all.

Tiffany Did you ever think he may have been protecting you?

Roger Why?

Tiffany Well, it's not for me to say, but you've not been a ball of fun yourself recently, have you? Maybe he didn't want to show you up with his extreme jubilance.

Maybe he thought you'd be angry at him for having such an absolute whale of a time.

Pause.

Roger I. I think I'll leave you. I'll leave you to it.

Tiffany Are you all right Mr Watson?

Roger Yeah. I'm sorry to have intruded on your . . . We'll talk tomorrow. It can wait. It can wait until tomorrow.

He exits upstairs, putting the cross the right way up as he goes. They extricate themselves. Peter wipes his hands and turns the cross back the wrong way round.

Peter Do you think he fell for it?

Tiffany I think so.

Peter Well done, Tiffany.

Tiffany Thanks.

Peter It's amazing what people will believe.

Tiffany What do you mean?

Peter I mean, I would have thought it obvious we have absolutely no romantic interest in each other whatsoever.

Tiffany Well, there you go.

Peter I mean, it's obvious to me. It's obvious to you, isn't it?

Tiffany Of course. It was just a story.

Peter A fabrication.

Tiffany A complete stony lie.

Peter As long as there's no confusion.

Tiffany Nothing could be clearer.

Peter And you had to hold my hand for realism purposes.

Tiffany I didn't want to.

Peter I don't want to make a big thing of it.

Tiffany I'm a professional.

Peter Did you have to squeeze it?

Tiffany It was a hand, Peter! That's all it was! This girl on Channel Five did a porn film with a triple entry and she didn't make half the fuss you are!

Roger returns down the stairs.

Roger Peter, I think there's a guest of yours up here.

Lynette comes down in an inconceivable dress.

Lynette All right?

Peter All right?

Roger She was in the bathroom.

Peter Was she?

Roger I'm Roger.

Lynette Lynette Seal. Charmed.

Roger I like your costume, Lynette. What movie does it come from?

Lynette It doesn't.

Beat.

Roger Are you a friend of Peter's?

Lynette We're only recently acquainted. And you?

Roger I'm Peter's father. I've surprised him by coming back.

Lynette You've surprised me. I thought you were dead.

Roger No, I'm not dead.

Lynette I thought Peter stabbed you to death.

Peter Why don't you go back to bed, Dad? We'll see Lynette out.

Roger I think I'll do that. Nice to meet you.

Lynette Likewise.

Exit Roger upstairs.

Peter What were you doing in our bathroom?

Lynette You didn't think I'd give in that easily, did you?

Peter How did you get in?

Lynette I followed you back here. Stayed out there in the darkness, in the rain. Biding my time like a puma. Then I saw my chance. The bathroom window was open. Well, I've had to shin up a few alley walls in my time. What do you think? (*of the dress*) I reckon one look at this, they won't be able to say no.

Tiffany Who is she?

Lynette I went into your bedroom. Either you've got a thing about Danny Crowe or you couldn't afford wallpaper.

Tiffany Who is she, Peter?

Lynette I'm the girl that's going on the show instead of you.

Peter I don't think so.

Lynette I will when I tell them that you've been telling porkies.

Peter We haven't.

Lynette Haven't you now?

Tiffany You don't know what you're talking about, you little slapper, so I suggest you shut your mouth.

Lynette Your dad's supposed to be huge and deceased. He's not very much of either.

Peter He can appear quite large when the mood strikes him.

Lynette You know what I reckon? I reckon you've made it all up because you don't have what it takes.

Peter No we haven't.

Lynette I reckon you're pretending to be a B minus so you can become an A plus, but actually you're just a D.

Peter No I'm not.

Lynette You're not even a D. You're off the scale you are.

Peter I am not!

Lynette Well then, you won't mind if I tell them. And when they hear you've been telling porkies, guess who gets promoted to the main slot?

Peter Why are you doing this?

Lynette It's nothing personal. I just need a break.

Peter Can't you wait your turn?!

Lynette What did you do last night? Shall I tell you what I did? Me and my colleague went to dinner with these two business blokes at the Travelodge on the bypass. They took us back to their room afterwards and we had a few drinks and extended a few physical courtesies. Then one of them said to Marie, he knew a special cocktail and would she like to try it? Well, she didn't know her own name by this point. And he held her mouth open and the other one pissed in it. And they kept shouting swallow the cocktail, swallow the cocktail. So sorry but I can't fucking wait, all right?

Peter Well, you're gonna have to.

Lynette We'll see about that, shall we?

Peter Yeah, we will.

Lynette What does that mean?

Peter It means this.

Tiffany grabs Lynette, who tries to scream, but Peter holds her mouth. She is still making noise so Tiff runs and pulls from a cupboard a CD player. She puts on 'Baby Hit Me One More Time' by Britney Spears, then rushes over and helps and they pin her down. Tiff grabs some tape from the kitchen and they bind her mouth and legs and arms, then push her through the window, and follow her out into the rain-sodden night.

Two

The stage is empty. The music is still playing.
  Roger comes down in his brown check pajamas. He goes to the music centre and turns it down. He stares at the room.

Roger Peter?

Roger shakes his head. He turns to go back up. He sees the cross. He turns it the right way up. He is on his way back up when the door bell rings.
  He approaches the door and is about to open it, when Peter crawls through the window.

Peter Aaah!

Roger Bleeding heck!

Peter What are you doing?

Roger I'm answering the door. What are you doing?

Peter Why are you answering the door?

Roger Because it rang.

Beat.

Peter I wouldn't bother.

Roger What?

Peter It'll be a latecomer for the party. We'll only have to send them away. It's a waste of your energy. (*The bell rings again.*) I tell you what. I'll get rid of them when you've gone back up. That way we can maximise your sleeping time.

Roger Are you embarrassed by me?

Peter Of course not.

Roger You are. You don't want them to meet me.

Peter It's not that.

Roger Don't lie to me. Why else would you have parties only when I go away? Why else shack up with Tiffany when I'm gone? Why else joke with that girl about killing me?

Peter I didn't. Honest!

Roger Then let me answer my own front door.

Peter (*barring the way*) I can't!

Roger Why not?

Peter Because . . . because . . . all right! I am embarrassed by you. I'm ashamed of you and I want as few of my many, many friends to meet you as humanly possible.

The bell rings again.

Dad, listen.

Roger No. It doesn't matter. I'm going up.

Peter Dad. I didn't mean . . .

Roger It doesn't matter! (*Beat.*) I'm going up. And Peter. About earlier. About my – show of emotion. You tell Tiffany. I'm just tired. She's not to go telling people.

Peter I'll tell her.

Roger I'm tired. It's been . . . I'm going up.

Roger goes upstairs. We hear a door close upstairs. Peter answers the front door. Miles enters on the phone.

Miles I'm here now, Danny. I'm walking in through the door. How long have I been doing this job? Well, I'm telling you, this is as grim as it gets. Social, emotional and moral desolation of the worst order. Yes, I think the word netherworld is very apt. What's that? Sure. Hold on.

He gives the phone to Peter

He wants to talk to you.

Pause as Peter takes the phone

Peter Hello? . . . (*to Miles*) It's just lots of drumming.

Miles He's learning tabla. Call out to him.

Peter Hello? . . . Yes, this is Peter. Thank you very much . . . how do I feel? Well, obviously desperate . . . needy . . .

Miles Crying out to be saved.

Peter Crying out to be saved . . . . Yeah, unfortunately she's a bit tied up right now.

Tiffany, a bit wet, rather muddy, enters through the window

No, she's here. She's here. (*Peter holds out the phone to Tiffany.*) He wants to talk to you.

Tiffany Who? (*Beat.*) Oh my God.

Peter Go on!

Tiffany Can't you say I'm on the loo?

Peter Tiffany!

Tiffany Danny? Oh my God, it's you. Oh God, I just think you're so fantastic, you're amazing, your heart must be so huge, how do you cope?

Miles takes the phone back

Miles What do you think? Yes, it's pretty bleak. Yes, really gets under the skin. So you want to go with this for the live special or not? (*Beat.*) OK. No, I think they're fine with that. We'll head off now. By the way, Danny. I've made a decision. After Monday, I don't want to do double shifts any more. It's affecting my work. Yes, let's close the file on Magda, shall we. I think we've all been waiting far too long.

Danny has rung off.

Peter He wants us on Monday?

Tiffany Live?

Miles It would seem so. Unless you want to wait . . .

Tiffany No! No.

Miles Why the mud?

Peter We were just saying a last farewell to Mum.

Miles Right.

Tiffany Shall we go then?

Miles has got out a camera and starts to take photos.

Peter What are you doing?

Miles Getting a sense of context. It helps Danny empathise. Peter, if you could stand by the sofa, this won't take a second. (*Miles starts to click a photoshoot of Peter looking miserable.*) You know your lives could change after this. Have you thought about that?

Peter Not in any depth.

Miles No, of course not. Could you slouch a bit more? Thanks. Well, there's the £200 appearance fee each for starters. And then, this is a show with ten million viewers. That means ten million potential fans. You catch on, you could be hot property. It all depends on whether they find you gripping. Gaze into the distance. Give it a tinge of class war. And then . . . Listen, I know this is the furthest thing from your mind rights now, but you should spend a little time considering the ramifications of a real hit – I mean there is the possibility of joining the circuit . . .

Peter/Tiffany Really?

Miles Well, that's nothing to worry about for now. Tiffany, just lean against that blood stain would you? (*Beat.*) There is one thing.

Peter What?

Miles We do need to come to an arrangement regarding Magda.

Peter Magda?

Miles She's bound to create a fuss when she realises what's happened

Tiffany Do you think so?

Miles I have a hunch she may, and I've been thinking about how we deal with that. This sounds extreme.

Tiffany Go on.

Miles I think it's best if we say you never met her.

Tiffany Will that work?

Miles No one knows she's here. She's written nothing down. She's told no one about you. It'll be her word against ours. Take a bit of advice from an old pro. Keep the story simple. I found you. I took you in.

Pause.

Look, I understand where you're coming from. She took pity on you and you respect her for that. But what's the bottom line? The bottom line is she can't deliver on her promises. She can't give you what you need. And I can't either if I'm not one hundred per cent sure that you will back me up on this.

Tiffany No problem.

Miles What about you, Peter?

Tiffany What about him?

Miles Peter may have become attached to Magda. It would be perfectly natural.

Tiffany No it wouldn't. And he hasn't. Have you Peter?

Peter Not remotely.

Miles So you'll say you never met her.

Peter Sure.

Miles And you'll never meet her again.

Peter Whatever you say.

Miles Good boy. I'll give you a hand with these.

Tiffany and Miles carry the first lot of stuff out of the front door. Peter thinks, leaps up, stops, sits, leaps up, grabs a piece of paper and writes a hurried letter. He is sticking it in an envelope when Tiffany re-enters.

Tiffany What's that?

Peter Nothing.

Tiffany Show me.

Peter It's just a letter for Dad.

Tiffany I thought we discussed it! No letters!

Peter A few brief words of farewell . . .

Tiffany Show me, Peter. Show me right now!

Peter, the letter behind his back, has circled the room but does not see Miles entering and approaching from behind. Miles takes it from him, reads the envelope and opens it.

Miles (*reading*) 'Dear Magda. By the time you read this letter I will be gone. I am sorry I must cast you aside but nothing must stand between me and my goals. I want you to know that what happened on Thursday night is branded deep in my heart. And that a part of me rests forever in you. Peter.'

Pause.

Tiffany What happened on Thursday night?

Peter . . .

Tiffany You said you were leading her on. You assured me you were leading her on!

Miles Why don't we talk about it in the car? (*Miles rips up the letter.*)

Tiffany I'm not going anywhere until he tells me what happened on Thursday night. (*Tiffany sits.*)

Pause.

Go on then.

Miles I don't want to hear this.

Tiffany Well I do!

Pause.

Peter It wasn't anything. We'd gone on late. She gave me a lift back. She stopped the car a few hundred yards before the house, as we always do, so he won't see the headlights. I was about to get out. And her hand sort of brushed my leg.

Tiffany Brushed it?

Peter Yeah.

Tiffany And that's it?

Peter Well, maybe it settled there for a while.

Tiffany Where did it settle?

Peter On the knee area.

Tiffany She touched your knee?

Peter Stroked might be a better word.

Tiffany And was it happy there or did it go walkies again?

Peter It may have strayed a little. I really don't remember.

Tiffany It's branded deep into your heart, Peter, how can you not fucking remember?!

Peter I think it found its way on to my chest. Then the other hand . . .

Tiffany I was wondering when that was going to make an appearance.

Peter The other hand seemed to leave the steering wheel and to very gently to caress my cheek. And then both hands worked together to move my head towards hers.

Pause.

Tiffany She kissed you. You bastard. How long for?

Peter Time really stopped for me at that point.

Tiffany You little lying bastard!

Peter You don't understand, Tiffany. She said she wanted to suck the pain out of me. She said I was a rare thing on this earth.

Tiffany And?

Peter She said . . .

Pause.

Miles What did she say?

Peter She said she felt a deep and very real love for me.

Miles She said what?

Tiffany You swore you were immune to all feeling. You said it was an investment that the modern man could not afford!

Peter Yeah, but she loves me, Tiffany.

Tiffany No she doesn't!

Peter No one has ever loved me like that.

Tiffany You don't know that.

Peter I do.

Tiffany No you don't! You don't know anything, you little prick!

Pause.

Miles Where are you going?

Tiffany I'm going for a walk.

Miles We have a deadline, young lady.

Tiffany I know all right! I am a ruthless operator with ice in my veins. I am going for a fucking walk! (*Exit Tiffany.*)

Pause.

Miles Shut it.

Peter I didn't say . . .

Miles Just shut it!

Pause.

Don't look at me.

Pause.

Don't look at me! What?

Peter Nothing. (*Pause.*) I just thought . . .

Miles What did you think?

Peter I thought it was over between you.

Miles And since when were you an expert on my relationship?

Peter That's just what she said. She said it was history.

Miles She told you about us?

Pause.

What did she say?

Peter She said you made each other unhappy.

Miles Did she? Right.

Peter She said that by the end you were both dead inside. There was something rotten in your relationship. As if a worm had found its way in and devoured your nerves.

Miles Right.

Peter She said that she was too full of needs and feelings. She said that very full people like her are drawn to empty people like you. She said it's as if their own fullness scares them, they need a dry sponge to soak it all up. But they don't realise that the sponge is in fact a desert that will receive and receive and never moisten. And then they realise they're drying up themselves.

Miles Right.

Peter They try to leave the desert but they can't find their way out. So they look to fill themselves back up from other sources. That's what Magda did. She started to throw herself into the show. She started to get too involved. She said you knew it was happening. And you encouraged it. Because it gave her the energy she needed to stay with you.

Miles Right, well, I think you're pretty much up to speed.

Peter Then she came here.

Miles Yes, I know what happened next! She came here and fell for you and your Greek fucking tragedy!

Peter Did you love her?

Miles Excuse me?

Peter Did you love her? Because I don't understand how if you loved her you could do that to another person. Make them suffer like that.

Miles Now you listen to me. You don't talk to me about suffering. You have no idea what I have been through in the last four months. No idea! (*Miles laughs.*) And now she's fallen for you. I mean, look at you. Ha ha ha. But you know what's really hilarious? I am taking you away from her. Because bottom line, and we must always remember the bottom line, bottom line is you don't love her at all. You love Danny Crowe. That's who we all love really.

Pause.

Now go and find your sister.

Exit Peter

I need a drink.

He searches but to no avail, only discovering binoculars and maps.

The man's a raging alcoholic, there has to be a drink somewhere.

He tries the huge cupboard but it is locked. He sees the cross, the right way up. He pauses. There is a knock at the door. He runs to open.
Magda enters. Pause

Miles Magda. You're early.

Magda What are you doing here?

Miles I was just passing.

Magda Where are they?

Miles They're . . . upstairs. Packing.

Magda What do you mean, you were just passing?

Pause.

Miles The truth is, I wanted to see you again. I've missed you so much. I didn't want to go without speaking to you one more time.

Magda Now?

Miles I know. I'll be off. It was a stupid idea.

Magda No, wait.

Miles Sorry?

Magda Go on then. Say what you were going to say.

Miles What, now?

Magda Why not? We have some time.

Miles Aren't you going to throw me out?

Magda Since you've had the honesty to come and talk to me, I think I owe you an audience.

Miles Right. Well, I just wanted to say that I'm sorry, for the way I behaved. And that I don't blame you for leaving me.

Magda What do you mean?

Miles Well, the fact is, and it took me a long time to realise this, I've been killing you. Yes. I'm an arid desert, taking your lifeforce, sucking it dry. You had no choice but to leave me.

Magda You have been doing some thinking.

Miles You're so full of life, Magda, you brim with it. You're like a geyser in spring. And I'm this empty vessel, hollow and cracked. But I want you to know that whatever you feel for me now, I will always be grateful to you for giving me the chance to understand what I'm like. And to try to change.

Magda You know this is really superb timing of yours.

Miles I know. It's crazy. Ha ha ha. But I had to say it.

Magda Why didn't you come before?

Miles Well, I hadn't fully grasped it until quite recently. (*looking out the front window*) Listen, it's getting late. I'm just wondering whether I should go and leave you with those lovely young people.

Magda Don't go yet. I want to say something.

Miles (*seeing something through the window but trying to hide it from Magda*) No, I think now might be the time for me to quit while ahead.

Magda What I said before isn't true.

Miles What isn't?

Magda I don't know if I want to be without you. I don't know what I want, Miles. I was so unhappy before I came here. I couldn't be in social situations. I couldn't look at people. I kept wanting to tear off their faces with my nails. I don't know if that was you, or me, or what it was. Since I've been here I've been able to breathe again. I feel free. But there hasn't been a day gone by when I haven't thought about . . .

Pause.

Miles Haven't thought about what?

Pause.

What? Tell me! For God's sake, Magda, tell me!

But Magda is looking at the floor and seeing the remnants of the letter. She picks them up as Miles fights her for them.

Miles Oh I wouldn't touch that if I were you.

Magda What is it?

Miles It's just something I wrote. Something to you. A crazy love letter. Wild ramblings of a diseased imagination.

Magda This isn't your handwriting.

Miles It is when I get overwrought. Why don't you give them to me?

Pause as Magda pieces together two or three of the bits of letter. She reads. She stares at Miles. A key in the door. Magda hides down in the sofa so that they can't see her. Peter and Tiffany enter. Tiffany has been crying.

Peter We're ready to go now, Miles.

Magda rises up.

Magda You lizard!

Miles I can explain.

Magda You're trying to steal my work.

Miles That is not true.

Magda Oh God! Oh God, how could I have fallen for it?

Miles Magda, you have to listen to me!

Magda What happened? Did you fake another show and get found out? (*Beat.*) Christ, you are a unique specimen.

Miles It's not my fault! I had some terrible luck!

Magda I don't want to know.

Miles As part of the great underbelly impetus, Danny wanted to tackle some serious weight issues. I had this idea about obese identical twins.

Magda I don't want to know!

Miles Because I was doubling for you, I didn't have time to traipse up and down the fucking country looking for them! I met these two actresses in a bar. They weren't identical, but they were similar, they were sizeable, they were happy to do the obese thing, happy to be padded, they knew a bit about it. No one would have known!

Magda Except?

Miles Except the bitches went on *Trisha* on Friday as divorcees! Danny fired me. He fired me on the fucking phone! Ten years I slaved for that cunt! I am not lying down to be shot like a fucking dog!

Magda So you thought you'd come and steal from me.

Miles I came here to win you back! That happened after. And even then if you hadn't been so viciously callous it could all have been all right!

Magda goes to the door

Magda Get out!

Miles No, wait. I can see a solution to all this. What were you going to say just now? There hasn't been a day where you haven't thought about . . . . About what? About me! Yes! About how we used to be! In the distant antique long-forgotten past! As I haven't spent a day, an hour, a minute without thinking about you, about your face, your skin!

Magda You destroyed me! You made me cold and indifferent. For the last year of our relationship I felt nothing!

Miles One year? Try thirty-five! I'm dead without you! You don't know what I've been going through! I tried to forget you. I went to bars and tried to chat up women. I couldn't open my mouth. I just stared at them with a kind of hate that I hoped was attractive but was actually just plain mad. When I did find someone too drunk and coked up to care, I couldn't do it. That's happened five times. I've lost my blood, Magda ! You are my blood!

Magda What about Danielle?

Miles There is no fucking Danielle! She was just a figment of your own neurotic fucking imagination!

Magda So who was she?

Miles She was Danny! She was always and always will be Danny! No, wait. Wait! I am not giving this up! I came to get you back and that is what I am going to do! Now listen! Listen! We go together, we give Danny his precious underbelly in the form of these two tormented young souls, and we leave. Yes! We leave everything! Don't you see? We can be different! We can be free! We can travel the world. We can live with the Latvian shepherds, buy a little cottage, become vegetable-growers and painters . . .

Magda Just go, Miles.

Miles I can't. I can't leave you.

Magda Please let me try to recover some dignity from all this.

Miles You think that's going to give you dignity?

Magda I need to achieve something. Something positive.

Miles The Danny Crowe special – one of the great moral contributions to the twenty-first century!

Magda I want to do something good. I want to try!

Miles Yeah, well, unfortunately I can't let you do that.

Magda What does that mean?

Miles I hate to tear lover boy away from you . . .

Magda He's not my lover.

Miles Well, maybe you neck all your potential guests in your car, maybe that's the way you work. It wouldn't entirely surprise me. (*to Peter*) You're not the first to have experienced the gift of Magda's deep and very real love, did you know that?

Magda That is not true!

Miles Oh yes? What about that guy on *I'm Dying and I'm Alone*. Cancer Man.

Magda His name was Bruce.

Miles Yup, Bruce! Let's talk about Bruce.

Magda I was helping Bruce die.

Miles Oh, please allow me a pause while I sanctify you.

Magda He came to the show with hope, hope of finding someone, anyone, to look after him. Danny left his Prozac in a taxi, the audience were animals, it was a farce! Someone had to help him!

Miles You wept at his funeral. You'd known him a week! People thought you were his wife! And now here you are washing the feet of the blackened boy from the wrong side of the tracks. Holding his tortured little soul in your healing hands. What are you – Mother fucking Theresa?!

Magda I've given my life for this project. I've gone without friends, gone without sleep, food, warmth . . .

Miles And you loved every second.

Magda He's mine! I found him! I nurtured him! I made him what he is!

Miles I mean, I am a twisted fucking piece of shit, but you are sick.

Magda I'm taking him.

Miles Yeah, sure you are.

Pause.

Well go on. What's stopping you?

Magda (*to Peter*) Come on, we're going.

Pause.

I said we're going. (*Beat.*) What's the problem?

Tiffany We believe Miles is the better option, that's what.

Magda How?

Tiffany In so many ways.

Magda I don't understand.

Tiffany And I'm in no mood for explanations.

Miles Magda, it's really very simple. You've got so much in your favour. Your deep and very real love for example. But there's one thing you're lacking, and it's proved fatal.

Magda What are you talking about?

Miles You don't have a job.

Magda You said you were covering for me.

Miles Not any more. My days of chivalry are over. And when I told Danny, he couldn't move fast enough to send you the P45. He loathes you, Magda. He goes mauve when he hears your name.

Magda That can change.

Miles Danny doesn't change. It's just not what he does.

Magda He will when I tell him what I've got. (*Magda starts to phone.*)

Miles I wouldn't do that.

Magda Oh, wouldn't you? (*She starts to dial.*)

Tiffany We'll deny we ever met you.

Magda What did you say?

Tiffany I mean, I'm just a rough underprivileged kid. What do I know of the intricacies of modern televisual politics? But the facts are here in front of my eyes. Besides being a liar and a slag, you're in no position to offer us the guarantees we need. Whereas Miles has already got us a whole hour on Monday.

Magda I can get you that.

Tiffany Can you though? You see Miles has already spoken to Danny, and as far as Danny's concerned, Miles is bringing in the show. To which I say, in my bluff Northern way, if it ain't broke . . .

Magda And what does Peter say?

Tiffany He says the same.

Magda Does he?

Tiffany Yes he fucking does!

Magda I want to hear that.

Miles You're not going to win this.

Magda (*she approaches Peter*) Peter, listen to me. You know you can trust me. You know how much I have given to this. You know how much I care for you.

Pause.

Peter The achievement of true celebrity requires three things. Discipline, discipline, discipline. Focus on the desired goal. Make success your friend. It's your party. Do not allow the gatecrasher doubt to enter. Remove from your mind all stains and blotches. Memories that impede you are burdens. Feelings that hold you back are shackles. Never in history has the ordinary man had such an opportunity to shine. Only his own weakness can ambush that opportunity. Only his own heart can stand in his way.

Magda What?

Peter I never met you, strange woman.

Magda I found you, you little shit.

Peter I don't know you. Now please stop hassling me and leave me alone.

Magda You're mine!

Peter Excuse me. I have a show to do.

Magda You're mine, you hear me!

Peter Someone get her off me.

Miles Let's get out of here.

Magda grabs the knife and blocks the door.

Magda No one leaves. No one leaves.

Miles Oh come on, Magda. You know you're not going to use that.

Miles approaches her but she swishes the blade and cuts his arm.

Miles Jesus! Jesus!

Magda Ha! I warned you.

Miles It cut me! It fucking cut me!

Magda What did you think it would do? Give you head?

Miles That's my blood! That's my fucking blood!

Magda It's a miracle you have any! Anyone else want some? You want some, bitch?

Tiffany Get out of my way.

Magda I found you, you little nothing. Without me you'd be still be in the dark ages!

Tiffany Get out of my way, whore!

Tiffany jumps Magda. A melee.

Suddenly a hand at the back window, tapping. A muddied finger pawing at the glass.

Magda It's him. It's the father.

Miles Keep away. Lock the doors. (*Beat.*) He's going to kill us.

Magda approaches the window.

What do you think you're doing?

Magda I'm letting him in.

Miles You're what?!

Magda That's what I mean. You always turn back just when things get interesting.

Magda goes to the window and opens. Lynette, soaked, taped up and covered in mud tumbles into the house. Her mouth is taped so she can only mumble her screams of fury. Magda untapes her.

Lynette Murderers! *Murderers!*

Magda I know you. You're . . .

Lynette I'm the girl who came here to turn a B minus into an A double-plus! I'm the girl they tied up in tape, dragged into the cemetery and tried to bury alive! Them! Myra Hindley and the other one! They poured earth over my body! I couldn't move my arms. I couldn't see through my eyes! All they left me was this tiny hole to breathe through! It was dark, I could feel the dead bodies stirring beneath me. I said Lynette you are beautiful inside and out! But there was this other voice saying, no, you're not Lynette, you've just been wrapped up and left for dead in a cemetery in the pissing rain. Focus on your inner window! I said. But the voice came back. You can't see! How can you focus on your inner window when you've got powdered corpse in your eyes! But I wouldn't allow the voice of negativity to get the better of me. I said, I am beautiful! Leave me for dead if you want, but I shall survive! So long as I learn how to love I know I'll stay alive! And as I sung the positivity mantra the tape loosened from my arms like the chains of negativity and the soil fell from my eyes like shame. I started to crawl through the grass, wriggling past gravestones, fighting, working, praying, I will make it through! The rain was soaking my clothes and the cold freezing my fingers but I kept going because I do not recognise the monster defeat! Past Elsie wife of Morris, past Byron much missed, past George Taverner and Robert Taverner brothers never parted not even by death. And then, like hope, a light through the trees. A light growing stronger and closer until it burst upon me like the grace of God himself! (*moving towards Peter*) You tried to destroy Lynette but Lynette was too strong. Now Lynette will destroy you. She will expose you to the world as the E minus nothing piece of shite you really are!

Peter tries to strangle her. Screams and fighting. Enter Mr Watson in his pajamas.

Roger Will you cut out that noise, I'm trying to sleep up here.

Pause.

What the bloody hell . . .

Miles Who are you?

Roger Who do you think I am?

Miles If I knew I wouldn't have asked, would I?

Roger I thought this party was over! (*Sees Lynette.*) What happened to you?

Lynette Your son tried to rub me out, that's what!

Magda (*to Lynette*) What did you say?

Lynette You heard.

Magda (*to Roger*) Who are you? Who are you?

Pause.

Roger I'm Peter's father.

Pause.

Peter He's not. Don't listen to him. He's always doing this. He's always coming round and claiming to be my father. It's really embarrassing.

Roger Peter, what are you saying?

Peter Listen, why don't you go home? I've just about had enough of you and your silly pranks. I don't want to see you here again. You're not my dad, you never were and you never will be. So just fuck off, weirdo!

Roger I demand to know what's going on in my house!

Peter It's not your house!

Roger Now you listen to me . . . I don't care what I've done, I do not deserve this.

Peter Honest, I don't know who he is.

Roger I've just about had enough for one night, you hear me? You go behind my back. You destroy my home. You deny my very existence.

Peter He's not my father. He's this lunatic who dogs innocent people claiming to be their long-lost parent.

Roger You're taking the rise, son!

Peter You think I'd have a father like him? Of his mediocrity? Of his blandness? You must be joking! My father's a colossus, morbid and fiery, with the fury of the devil and the weakness of a child. (*to Roger*) I tell you what, when my real dad gets back, be afraid. Be very afraid!!

Roger Peter, stop this. Please stop this.

Tiffany I think we should go, Miles. This guy's wasting our time.

Miles I want to know who this prick is.

Roger I have no idea who you are but let me tell you something. I don't like you at all.

Miles Then I'll tell you who I am. I am Miles Trafford. I work for a television company. And if you don't shut your stupid Northern mouth, I will dedicate the next five series to destroying your life!

Roger Television company. What television company?

Miles That is no concern of yours.

Roger You're not from . . . no, you couldn't be.

Pause.

No. You couldn't be.

Miles Couldn't be what?

Pause.

Roger You're not from . . .

Pause.

Roger Oh no. Oh son.

Peter I'm not your son, I don't know you and I'm due at a very important occasion in London.

Roger Oh son.

Peter Let's go to London! To London!

Roger Oh son, what have you done?

Roger walks to the big cupboard door. He finds the key in a drawer and unlocks the cupboard and opens it. It is large, and jam-packed with video tapes and a huge modern television. All the tapes have 'Danny Crowe Show' written on the side, with numbers from 1 to 487.

Magda What is that?

Roger Peter's library.

Miles His what?

Roger He watches them, he records them, he watches them again and again and again. He studies them as you would a book.

Pause as Miles reads the tapes

Miles 'Divorced But Still Doing It', 'My Sister Is My Mother', 'Romance Behind Bars', 'I Want To Be A Woman', 'I Am Dying And I'm Alone'.

Roger Tiffany, will you please tell me what is going on here?

Tiffany It's a bit complicated, Mr Watson.

Magda Who is she?

Roger Tiffany is Peter's best friend.

Magda She's not your daughter?

Roger No, she's Brian and Jill Longthorne's girl.

Magda But your wife . . .

Roger What about my wife?

Magda Where is she?

Roger My wife left us five years ago.

Magda Died.

Roger Died?

Magda Not dead?

Roger No, of course she's not bloody dead. Who said she was dead?

Pause.

Miles Oh, you little bastard.

Miles tries to get to Peter. Tiffany fights him off.

Tiffany Get off him!

Miles Why would I get off him? I want to fucking murder him!

Tiffany I said get off him!

Miles Get out of my way! (*He throws her out of the way and confronts Peter.*)

Peter Danny is love. He is truth. This is all patchwork and he is wholeness. Everything's in ruins, but he can make it fit. I know that one day he will come! He will come and get me. He will come and fetch me for I am in hell and my place is up there in the gods beside him! He will come and take me and make me shine!

Miles What are you talking about?

Peter You don't know because you are just a messenger! But I have watched and I have seen people's lives turned from despair to delight by one touch of his hand. I have seen miracles! I have seen healing! I want that! I want the touch of that hand on my forehead! I want that love! I have a right to that love! I have a right! (*Peter is having an asthma attack.*)

Roger Peter?

Tiffany Peter, are you all right?

Miles What's this?

Magda I'll tell you what it is. It's a new routine.

Tiffany tries to get to him. Magda wards her off with the knife. Magda stands between him and the rest, wielding the knife.

Don't you get it, Miles? It's another performance.

Tiffany No, he's got a condition. He needs his thingy.

Magda (*to Peter*) If this is a desperate last-ditch attempt to rescue something from this mess, let me tell you. It won't work. Gasp all you like, you get nothing from me.

Roger runs to the basket and gets the inhaler. Magda blocks the way.

Magda Don't touch him!

Tiffany He can't breathe! He's dying!

Magda Then let him. I want to see it! (*to Peter*) And then you know what I'll do, you little fucker? I'll take your corpse in my car, drive it to the studio and I'll put it on that fucking sofa and I'll interview you my fucking self!

Roger Get away from him. I mean it.

Pause. Magda turns. Roger has the inhaler in his hand.

Magda Don't try it, little man.

Roger My son is having an asthma attack and I am going to help him. Now get out of my way.

Roger tries to wrestle the knife from Magda, there is a fight, they close together. Pause. Magda and Roger draw apart. He staggers away with the knife sticking in his upper chest. Tiffany and Lynette scream.

Tiffany Oh my God.

Lynette Oh wow. Oh fucking wow.

Peter Dad!

Tiffany Oh my fucking God. Oh my God!

Roger It's all right.

Tiffany Oh God.

Roger It's all right.

Tiffany runs to the phone and dials.

Tiffany This is 24623. Seven, Mahon Cottages. We need an ambulance! He's been stabbed. He's been stabbed! We need a fucking ambulance!

Peter, still wheezing heavily, approaches his father who is holding his chest tight.

Peter Dad?

Roger It's all right.

Peter I'm sorry, Dad.

Roger It's OK. I'll be OK.

Peter I didn't mean to cause any trouble.

Roger You haven't. You haven't.

Peter It's bull's blood. It comes off.

Roger Sshhh, it's all right.

Peter It all comes off.

Roger Ssshh.

Peter Don't be angry. Please don't be angry.

Roger I'm not angry.

Pause.

It's not a case of . . .

Pause.

It's not a case . . .

Long pause as Roger sits dead still on the sofa.

There are no crematorium awaydays.

Pause.

Every month, I take a train to Crewe. I change there and catch a train to Stockport. There's a fast service from Stockport that takes me to Grimsby. I walk to her house. There's a phone box opposite. I hide in it and look through her window. I see them get up. They have a baby, I watch them wash it, change nappies, do the things you do. Sometimes if the baby's crying he takes it out in the car. I've thought about knocking. I never have. I watch her brushing her hair. It's much shorter now. She looks well – she's still only thirty-six. But she's flowered.

They go for a walk in the park. There's a pond where they feed the ducks. Baby's in a push-pram. They sit by the pond, hold each other's hand and chat. Angie's got an old red scarf on, it's one we bought in Sheffield when you were small. The rest of her clothes are new. She leans her head on his shoulder. He's taller than her, he's wearing a soft blue coat, and her head fits perfectly. She rests it there and he whispers in her ear. She laughs, she kisses his neck. She kisses his neck and her fingers play with the hair on the back of his head.

They caught me once before. I pretended it was the first time, swore I'd never come again. I've been more careful since. But today, I had to see the baby's face. I had to know what sex it was. I don't even know that. He saw me. He said I was a pervert. I was ruining their life. Couldn't I see that they wanted to be left alone? I asked if she was happy. She said happier than she'd ever believed possible. I looked at the baby. You can't tell from the face, can you – the sex I mean. You just can't tell.

I came home. Found all this. I went upstairs. I stood there for a long time. I don't think I would have done it but sometimes when it gets like that, you just don't know anything.

Peter Why didn't you tell me?

Roger Well, it's sick isn't it?

The sound of a distant ambulance in the night. Tiffany runs to the door.

Peter Did she . . . did she ask after me?

Pause.

Roger She did. She did.

Peter Did she?

Roger She did. She did.

Peter What did she say?

Roger There wasn't much time . . .

Peter But she said something.

Roger She said hello.

Peter Did she?

Roger She did. She said to say hello.

Peter Did she?

Roger She did. She did.

The ambulance is moving closer and closer. Suddenly it stops. Miles' phone rings.

Miles Hello Danny. How's the meditation?
You quit. I see.
No, we're still here.
There's been a development.
Listen to this and tell me what you think.

End.

*Discover the brightest and best in fresh theatre writing
with Faber's new StageScripts*

Sweetheart by Nick Grosso (0571 17967 3)
Mules by Winsome Pinnock (0571 19022 7)
The Wolves by Michael Punter (0571 19302 1)
Gabriel by Moira Buffini (0571 19327 7)
Skeleton by Tanika Gupta (0571 19339 0)
The Cub by Stephanie McKnight (0571 19381 1)
Fair Game by Rebecca Prichard (0571 19476 1)
(a free adaptation of **Games in the Backyard** by Edna Mazya)
Crazyhorse by Parv Bancil (0571 19477 x)
Sabina! by Chris Dolan (0571 19590 3)
I Am Yours by Judith Thompson (0571 19612 8)
Been So Long by Che Walker (0571 19650 0)
Yard Gal by Rebecca Prichard (0571 19591 1)
Sea Urchins by Sharman Macdonald (0571 19695 0)
Twins by Maureen Lawrence (0571 20065 6)
Skinned by Abi Morgan (0571 20007 9)
Real Classy Affair by Nick Grosso (0571 19592 x)
Down Red Lane by Kate Dean (0571 20070 2)
Shang-a-Lang by Catherine Johnson (0571 20077 x)
The Storm by Alexander Ostrovsky
trs. Frank McGuinness (0571 20004 4)
By Many Wounds by Zinnie Harris (0571 20097 4)
So Special by Kevin Hood (0571 20044 3)
The Glory of Living by Rebecca Gilman (0571 20140 7)
Certain Young Men by Peter Gill (0571 20191 1)
Paddy Irishman, Paddy Englishman and Paddy . . . ?
by Declan Croghan (0571 20128 8)
Pelleas and Melisande by Maurice Maeterlinck
trs. Timberlake Wertenbaker (0571 20201 2)
Martha, Josie and the Chinese Elvis
by Charlotte Jones (0571 20237 3)
My Best Friend by Tamsin Oglesby (0571 20566 6)
Dogs Barking by Richard Zajdlic (0571 20006 0)
All That Trouble That We Had by Paul Lucas (0571 20267 5)
The Bedsit by Paul Sellar (0571 20364 7)
Drink, Dance, Laugh and Lie by Samuel Adamson (0571 20442 2)
The Map Maker's Sorrow by Chris Lee (0571 20365 5)
Silence by Moira Buffini (0571 20445 7)
Bitter with a Twist by Simon Treves (0571 20479 1)
My Dad's Corner Shop by Ray Grewal (0571 20534 8)
Jump Mr Malinoff, Jump by Toby Whithouse (0571 20584 4)
The Waiting Room by Tanika Gupta (0571 20514 3)
Still Time by Stephanie McKnight (0571 20782 0)
The Slight Witch by Paul Lucas (0571 20935 1)
Behind the Scenes at the Museum by Bryony Lavery (0571 20911 4)
A Wedding Story by Bryony Lavery (0571 20906 8)
Belonging by Kaite O'Reilly (0571 20902 5)